COOL CAREERS
WITHOUT COLLEGE
FOR PEOPLE WHO LOVE
PHOTOGRAPHY

MARCIA AMIDON LUSTED

ROSEN
PUBLISHING®

New York

Published in 2017 by The Rosen Publishing Group, Inc.
29 East 21st Street, New York, NY 10010

Library of Congress Cataloging-in-Publication Data

Names: Lusted, Marcia Amidon, author.
Title: Cool careers without college for people who love photography.
Description: First edition. | New York : Rosen Publishing, 2017. | Series:
  Cool careers without college | Audience: Grades 7-12. | Includes
  bibliographical references and index.
Identifiers: LCCN 2016017411 | ISBN 9781508172765 (library bound)
Subjects: LCSH: Photography—Vocational guidance—Juvenile literature.
Classification: LCC TR154 .L87 2017 | DDC 770.23—dc23
LC record available at https://lccn.loc.gov/2016017411

Manufactured in China

CONTENTS

INTRODUCTION

Before students even reach high school, they are often asked to decide on possible careers. Everyone hopes to have a career doing something that he or she cares about or is interested in. The best careers are those that people are passionate about. A job that you can't wait to start every morning is more than just a job.

However, few careers happen without education and training. Many careers require at least four years of college and sometimes more for occupations like medicine and law. With the cost of college rising every year, many students don't want to take on the huge amount of debt that is now necessary to complete a degree that will get them a job. Fortunately, not every career requires huge amounts of tuition money or four or more years of college. There are other options for learning a career. They include vocational programs that start during high school, apprenticeships in trades like plumbing and electricity, or on-the-job training with additional education paid for by the employer. There are also community colleges, which are often geared to two-year programs in careers like health care or training in computers or mechanical trades. Community colleges

Working as a professional photographer means not only knowing how to use your camera and other equipment but also understanding what makes good photographs and how to create them.

typically cost much less than regular colleges, and they can equip students to start working with a degree or certificate in their chosen profession after just a few years.

For students who don't know exactly what they want to do for a career and don't want to spend money on college until they have a better idea of their aspirations, sometimes the best place to start is with hobbies and interests. What is it that you're good at? What do you like to do for fun? What are your hobbies? Can any of these translate into a career? Happily, the answer is usually yes. There are many interests that can become jobs and careers. And if you are someone who loves to take pictures and is good at using a camera, then there are many options that can be a good fit for you, without college or special training programs.

The career options for people who like to use cameras range from traditional portrait photography to unusual types of photography such as scientific or forensic photography. Photographers might take photos of industrial machinery or models. Or they might take aerial photographs from helicopters. Perhaps they travel around the world to provide photos for travel magazines and websites or to document a war or disaster for news outlets. Many of these careers do not require college or even formal training. Often what it takes is the knack to use a camera for interesting photographs, as well as the willingness to learn on the job and through experience.

If these jobs sound intriguing, it's time to get started. In this book, you will learn about ten different careers for people who are good at using cameras. Each chapter talks about the job itself, as well as how to prepare for the job with courses and training, starting in high school. It will also explain the best places to find these jobs and if the opportunities are growing for working in that field. There are also resources for more information.

CHAPTER 1

PHOTOJOURNALIST

In the pages of glossy magazines or on the front pages of major newspapers, there are often dramatic photographs of people, places, and events that are in the news at that moment. These photographs accompany a news story and illustrate what is taking place. These photos are the job of a news photographer.

There is also another type of news photograph. These are images that tell a story by themselves, with little text. They are usually of dramatic, newsworthy events, like a riot taking place or the aftermath of a natural disaster. Instead of simply taking an ordinary photograph, the photographer tries to get shots that are dangerous, difficult, or unusual. They are intended to make the viewer feel intense emotions. The person who takes these photos is a photojournalist. Unlike news photographers,

In the 1930s, news photographers were documenting history with the rise of Hitler and the Nazi Party in Germany. Before the era of television, photographers were the only way for most people to see pictures of world events.

they tell stories through images instead of providing photos to support a written story.

A DAY IN THE LIFE

What tasks does a photojournalist have to do for his or her job? It depends on the location and the event being photographed, but they always include:

- Traveling to the location of the event
- Carrying equipment, including digital and film cameras (in some parts of the world, digital cameras are not easily charged), lighting, batteries, and chargers
- Finding the best angles and subjects for the photographs, which may involve finding a position that is safe but still captures vivid action
- Interviewing subjects of photographs
- Returning home to download or develop photographs
- Selling photographs to a news organization or publisher or compiling them into a book that can then be marketed and sold
- Seeking photojournalism assignments from media organizations

Most photojournalists are freelancers, meaning that they do not work for one company. Instead, they sell their photographs to publications, so they must spend time

Being out in the field taking photographs is just one part of being a photojournalist. It helps to be bold and unafraid of taking risks.

A CAREER AND A CALLING

Lynsey Addario is a photojournalist. She spends her life taking photographs that have been called "vivid," "haunting," and "informative." Addario has been covering wars in the Middle East for twenty years. As a woman, she is allowed to access women in those cultures, which is something that male photojournalists are not allowed to do. Her work is often dangerous and difficult. She was once embedded with a group of American soldiers and photographed the death of one soldier, who was her friend. Addario believes that photojournalism is about much more than taking pictures. "I think when I started going to war zones and started covering humanitarian issues it became a calling because I realized I had a voice, and I can give people without a voice a voice... and now it is something that sits inside of me every day," she told CBS News.

marketing their photos and seeking new assignments for future photography opportunities. Photojournalism is a fast-paced career, with frequent travel to often unsafe places, and these photographers must be in good physical shape, have good timing, and be ready to do anything they need to in order to get their photos. They also need to be persistent in getting interviews and photo opportunities even in places where they might be restricted. It helps to be fearless and also to know that a photojournalism career can be stressful and emotionally draining.

Photojournalists may find themselves in dangerous and hostile situations, such as documenting a war as it is taking place around them on a battlefield.

WHAT EDUCATION AND TRAINING DO PHOTOJOURNALISTS NEED?

Becoming a photojournalist does not always mean getting a college degree, although some photojournalists do earn degrees in journalism. Others simply learn on the job, often by working for a news organization assisting another photojournalist and then being sent on increasingly dangerous assignments on their own. Students interested in photojournalism should start by taking courses in photography in high school to learn about equipment, the process of taking photos, and techniques. For future freelance photojournalists, high school classes in business or accounting can also be useful.

JOB OUTLOOK

As a career, photojournalism is growing more slowly than the average for all jobs. It is a very competitive field, and since print newspapers and magazines are declining in popularity, there are not as many opportunities to achieve a full-time job working for a news organization. However, with internet and social media growing in popularity, they will always provide markets for vivid photographs of current events.

FOR MORE INFORMATION

BOOKS

Buell, Hal. *Moments: The Pulitzer Prize-Winning Photographs*. New York, NY: Black Dog & Leventhal, 2015.
This book showcases Pulitzer Prize–winning news photographs.

Keene, Martin. *Practical Photojournalism: A Professional Guide*. London, UK: Ammonite Press, 2016.
The author, who worked as a photojournalist for forty years, provides practical advice for how to take news photos and establish a career.

Kobre, Kenneth. *Photojournalism: The Professionals' Approach*, 6th ed. New York, NY: Focal Press, 2008.
This book is a how-to about photojournalism and also takes the reader along on actual jobs with real photojournalists.

PERIODICALS

News Photographer Magazine
National Press Photographers Association
120 Hooper Street
Athens, GA 30602-3018
Website: https://nppa.org/magazine

News Photographer magazine supports the National Press Photographers Association by communicating news and trends and recognizing the work of photojournalists.

BLOG

Lens: Photography, Video, and Visual Journalism blog from the *New York Times*
Website: http://lens.blogs.nytimes.com
Lens is the photojournalism blog of the *New York Times*, showing the finest and most interesting visual reporting, including photographs, videos, and slide shows.

WEBSITES

Because of the changing nature of internet links, Rosen Publishing has developed an online list of websites related to the subject of this book. This site is updated regularly. Please use this link to access this list:

http://www.rosenlinks.com/CCWC/camer

CHAPTER 2

STUDIO PHOTOGRAPHER

Everyone loves those casual photographs that are snapped on phones and cameras every day. But there are times in everyone's lives when they want a more formal photograph of themselves or their family. At those times, they visit a photography studio and have their photograph taken by a studio photographer. Basically, it is the job of studio photographers to preserve memories.

Studio photographers are photographers who remain in one location where customers come to them. While studio photographers might leave the studio once in a while, perhaps to take photographs of a wedding or other special event, they do most of their work in their studio. Being in one location means that they can create backdrops and settings for their portraits that wouldn't be possible to do in the real world without travel and other complications. By using artificial backdrops, studio lights, and even special costumes, studio photographers can help portray a specific feeling or idea. They can also control the lighting and don't

Some studio photographers specialize in fashion photography. They work with models and take a large number of photos of them in different poses and outfits.

have to worry about weather, time of day, and other factors that can impact the quality of a photograph.

Studio photographers can also create artistic portraits of their subjects. They try to convey the mood, expression, or personality of their subject, usually focusing just on the face. If they are doing a formal photograph of a bride, however, they need to be able to show her gown and use lighting to make the image soft and romantic. If they are photographing a family, they may try to show relationships by grouping

A VOICE FROM THE FIELD

Deb Blair is a photographer living in Oregon. She does wedding and family photography, as well as scenic photographs. But she got her start when she was still in high school. "I bought my first camera at age 13 with money I earned babysitting. I knew I liked to take photos, so in high school, I signed up to take photos for the school newspaper and yearbook and in my senior year did some senior photos for friends," Blair said. "Unfortunately, there were no photography classes offered while I was in high school or at the college I attended. I was fortunate to have one of my school teachers teach me how to process black and white film." Her advice to students interested in photography careers? "Practice. Carry your camera with you wherever you go and don't be afraid to experiment and to try new angles and perspectives. Digital photography has opened my eyes to experimenting because the number of shots are limitless."

subjects in certain ways. Studio photographers may also be photographing babies and young children. They need to know how to work with their young subjects, to get their attention and get them to smile. They may also have special props to use with babies and children.

A DAY IN THE LIFE OF A STUDIO PHOTOGRAPHER

What tasks do studio photographers do in the course of a regular day? It depends on whom they are photographing, but those tasks usually include:

- Using marketing and advertising to attract clients
- Ordering supplies, keeping records, paying bills, and sending invoices for payment
- Analyzing and planning the best way to compose (set up) photographs
- Setting up lighting, backgrounds, and other equipment
- Using various photographic techniques and lighting to take commercial-quality photographs
- Enhancing the subject's appearance with natural or artificial light
- Using editing software to enhance or correct photographs after taking them
- Maintaining a digital portfolio, usually on a website, to demonstrate their work

- Traveling to special locations, such as a school or a wedding, to take photographs

Most studio photographers run their own businesses so they must maintain the business side of their studio as well

One of the most important aspects of getting a good studio photograph is having the proper setup and use of lighting. Lighting can create or change the mood of the photo and enhance the quality of the image.

Many photographers get their start in high school, photographing sporting events and other activities or taking candid shots for their school's yearbook or newspaper.

as simply taking photographs. This includes billing, invoices, purchasing equipment and supplies, and sometimes hiring and training employees. Some studio photographers work for national studio franchises, which are companies that operate photo studios all over the country. Others might work for a large department store in their photography studios. These photographers have fewer administrative responsibilities since they are employees rather than business owners.

WHAT EDUCATION AND TRAINING DO STUDIO PHOTOGRAPHERS NEED?

Some studio photographers, especially those who do formal portrait or artistic photography, attend college and receive two- or four-year degrees. Others have a basic knowledge of photography and cameras but receive their training on the job. They might be employed as assistants in a portrait studio, working with more experienced photographers. Others might be hired by a store photography studio and receive less formal training, learning most of what they need to know as they work.

Anyone who is interested in working as a studio photographer can begin by taking photography courses in high school. These should include photography courses on the basics of how cameras work and how to use lighting. He

FOUR-LEGGED SUBJECTS

There are photography studios and photographers who specialize in nonhuman subjects. Special studios for photographing beloved pets like dogs and cats, or even horses, are increasingly popular. For large animals like horses, the photographer generally has to travel to a location to take photographs. But many studios welcome smaller pets and know how to set up and take great photographs of sometimes uncooperative subjects. Pet photographers usually require at least one assistant to help them by handling the animal. They use treats to get the animals to cooperate, as well as limiting distractions in the room. Photographers must also be patient, and of course, it helps if they really love animals.

or she should also take art courses in composition and art survey classes of famous photography and photographers. Volunteering to take photographs for the school yearbook is also a way to become comfortable with taking portraits of people and groups.

JOB OUTLOOK

While the job growth for all photographers is expected to be slower than most other jobs, studio photographers are expected to see a higher rate of growth. This is simply because people will always want professional photographs for special events and memories. Since these kinds of photographs require professional expertise in lighting and photograph composition, studio photographers are still in demand even though digital photography has made it easier for people to take and edit their own photographs.

FOR MORE INFORMATION

BOOKS

Dallas, Justin. *Fashion Photographer: The Coolest Jobs on the Planet*. Hampshire, UK: Raintree, 2014.
A look at what it's really like to work in a studio as a fashion photographer.

Gatcum, Chris. *The Beginner's Photography Guide*. New York, NY: DK Publishing, 2013.
This book introduces the equipment and techniques for taking good photographs.

MacGregor, Hanna. *Portrait Photography: The Essential Beginner's Guide*. London, UK: Ammonite Press, 2015.
A complete guide for beginners on shooting good portrait photographs.

ORGANIZATIONS

American Photography Association
PO Box 951777
Lake Mary, FL
(407) 536-4611
Website: www.americanphotographyassociation.org
An association for all photographers, of every type and skill level.

Professional Photographers of America

229 Peachtree Street NE, Suite 2200
Atlanta, GA 30303
(800) 786-6277
Website: http://www.ppa.com
This association for professional photographers focuses
    on wedding, studio, and portrait photography.

Wedding and Portrait Photographers International
Emerald Expositions
85 Broad Street, 11th Floor
New York, NY 10004
Website: http://www.wppionline.com
This organization is dedicated to the needs of wedding
    and portrait photographers.

PERIODICALS

Studio and Location Photography
1233 Janesville Avenue
Fort Atkinson, WI 53538
(631) 963-6200
Website: http://www.imaginginfo.com/publication/
index.jsp?pubId=3
This photography magazine focuses on photographers
    as small business owners, with advice on marketing,
    business, and techniques.

WEBSITES

Because of the changing nature of internet links, Rosen Publishing has developed an online list of websites related to the subject of this book. This site is updated regularly. Please use this link to access this list:

http://www.rosenlinks.com/CCWC/camera

CHAPTER 3

SPECIALIZED STUDIO PHOTOGRAPHER

Every Christmas and Easter, Santa and the Easter Bunny occupy malls across America. Parents often take their children to meet them and to pose for photos. A professional photographer is there to capture those moments and try to get the best shots despite screaming children and lots of distractions.

In schools and universities, there are also professional photographers who come once or twice a year to take those school photos that almost everyone gets to chronicle their progression through school. They also take yearbook photos, senior portraits, and other graduation portraits. There are also photographers who photograph student-athletes. They sometimes produce photographs that look like trading cards, taken on the playing field or in a gym or other sports facility.

Another area for professional photographers is newborn photography, which is usually done in hospitals, as well as photography done for church directories and other organizations, also usually done on site.

Finally, there are wedding and engagement photographs that most couples want as part of their marriage celebrations. The photographer must not only travel to the site of the wedding but also sometimes to scenic locations where engagement photos might be taken.

What do all these types of jobs have in common? They require the expertise and talent of a professional studio photographer, but they also involve the challenges of working outside of a studio, in conditions that may not be the best. These kinds of photography are a logistical challenge, getting equipment to where it is needed and possibly dealing with bad weather. They can also be a personal challenge, trying to manage large groups of people, often during exciting events.

A DAY IN THE LIFE OF A SPECIALIZED STUDIO PHOTOGRAPHER

Like studio photographers, many of the daily tasks that specialized photographers do are related to running a business, like keeping records, invoicing, and ordering supplies and equipment. But there are additional tasks related to the traveling nature of their jobs.

- Setting up backdrops and any special props
- Setting up group shots and making sure that there is a record of names of the people in the photographs

Many photographers specialize in taking photographs of newborn babies. It takes skill and patience to work with babies and children, who may not always cooperate when they have their photos taken.

Since many weddings are held outside, most wedding photographers like to see the venue in advance so that they can plan the best angles and backgrounds for photographs.

- Keeping a schedule of groups and events (in a school setting) or of individual appointments for sittings (for individual photographs)
- Visiting a wedding venue in advance to be prepared with the right equipment for the location, as well as composing some of the shots that will be needed
- Making sure that everyone who needs to be photographed has been
- Using a content management system to keep track of and identify people in photographs

- Using editing software to enhance or adjust photographs
- Meeting with customers to show and select photographs for printing. Some photographers who work in school settings may hire an assistant to manage scheduling and timing for photo shoots. This is especially important if a large number of students need to be photographed on a tight schedule. This means that the photographer has to hire and train the assistant and schedule his or her time. If the photographer is employed by a larger company, such as a school portrait company, this may be done for him or her.

WHAT EDUCATION AND TRAINING DO SPECIALIZED STUDIO PHOTOGRAPHERS NEED?

As with any studio photographer, it may be necessary to attend college and receive a two- or four-year degree. But a basic knowledge of photography and cameras may be all that's needed, and on-the-job experience will perfect skills. Photographers who are employed through a larger company, such as one that specializes in school portraits and yearbook publishing, will receive much of their training through the company's training programs, as well as on the job. They will learn the procedures and skills needed to do their job professionally.

Anyone who is interested in working as a photographer can begin by taking photography courses in high school. These should include photography courses that teach the basics of how cameras work and how to use lighting. Volunteering to take photographs for the school yearbook is even more helpful, and it is also a way to become comfortable with taking portraits of people and groups. Some photography jobs, such as those that are temporary holiday positions at malls and in department stores, can provide valuable experience in dealing with the factors involved with young children and distracting settings.

JOB OUTLOOK

The job outlook for a specialized studio photographer is the same as that for a regular studio photographer. While the job growth for all photographers is expected to be slower than most other jobs, studio photographers are expected to see a higher rate of growth. This is simply because people will always want professional photographs for special events and memories. Often school and team photos, as well as those for yearbooks, cannot be taken by amateur photographers because they do not have access to those locations and subjects.

UNUSUAL PLACES

Wedding photographers don't always end up photographing ceremonies in churches or gardens. Being a wedding photographer might mean traveling to a museum, a converted historic building, a famous library or theater, a boat traveling around a lake or down a river, a tree house, or even a hot-air balloon! Wedding locations are becoming more exotic as couples no longer feel the need to get married inside churches or other houses of worship. Some couples even get married in extreme locations, such as volcanoes, glaciers, mountaintops, or in the air while skydiving. A wedding photographer with a sense of adventure and the ability to travel and take good photos in unusual circumstances can find a niche in photographing these kinds of weddings.

Some weddings take place in unusual locations, and wedding photographers may need to cope with very challenging conditions while still capturing great photos.

FOR MORE INFORMATION

BOOKS

Fancher, Nick. *Studio Anywhere: A Photographer's Guide to Shooting in Unconventional Locations.* San Francisco, CA: Peachpit Press, 2015.
This book provides tips and techniques for taking good-quality photographs in unusual or difficult situations.

Florens, Brett. *One Wedding: How to Photograph a Wedding from Start to Finish.* Amherst, MA: Amherst Media, 2014.
A step-by-step guide to photographing a wedding, including technical tips and time management advice.

Hyde, Lena. *The Design Aglow Posing Guide for Family Portrait Photography: 100 Modern Ideas for Photographing Newborns, Babies, Children, and Families.* New York, NY: Amphoto Books, 2013.
This book provides one hundred specific poses as well as advice for posing babies, children, and families for photographs.

Vayo, Ellie. *The Art and Business of High School Senior Portrait Photography,* 2nd ed. Amherst, MA: Amherst Media, 2013.

This book provides valuable information, including pricing and marketing, for succeeding as a high school portrait photographer.

ORGANIZATIONS

Wedding & Portrait Photographers International (WPPI)
85 Broad Street, 11th Floor
New York, NY 10004
Website: http://www.wppionline.com
An organization that provides support and a community for wedding photographers around the world.

Youth Sports Photography Network Connection (YSPNC)
National Council of Youth Sports
7185 S.E. Seagate Lane
Stuart, FL 34997
Website: http://ncys.org/safety/yspnc.php
The youth sports organization that promotes KidSafe photography partnerships, creating safety for child-athletes.

PERIODICALS

Photographer's Forum
Serbin Communications, Inc.
813 Reddick Street
Santa Barbara, CA 93103
(800) 876-6425
Website: http://pfmagazine.com
A magazine for emerging professional photographers in
   all genres.

BLOG

Fearless Photographers
Website: http://www.fearlessphotographers.com/blog
A wedding photography blog for brides, grooms, and
   photographers.

WEBSITES

Because of the changing nature of internet links, Rosen
Publishing has developed an online list of websites
related to the subject of this book. This site is updated
regularly. Please use this link to access this list:

http://www.rosenlinks.com/CCWC/camera

CHAPTER 4

MUSIC VIDEO PRODUCER

Being good with a camera isn't just limited to still photography. For people who like to make videos, there are even more career options, and one of the most interesting ones is to make and produce music videos. Those two- or three-minute videos that end up on television, YouTube, and websites are fast, flashy, and fun. They are basically advertising for the musician or group, and while music channels like MTV aren't using nearly as many videos as they once did, they are still needed.

Music video producers are the ones who coordinate all the aspects of making a video: cast, director, and production crew. They must stay within the budget they are given, negotiate contracts with the people working for them, make schedules and meet deadlines, and generally make sure that the whole process goes as smoothly as possible. They must also manage the sometimes tricky relationship with the musical artists they are making the videos with, as well as their agents, which isn't usually as glamorous as it sounds.

According to an article on CFNC.org, "You'd better like working with people. Producers are the ones who bring together all the creative and technical people involved with making a video. This means they can sometimes be dealing with difficult people and big egos."

A DAY IN THE LIFE OF A MUSIC VIDEO PRODUCER

Working as a producer of music videos requires several different stages, from organizing to shooting to editing. A typical day might include:

- Creating a script or storyboard for an upcoming video
- Setting up a schedule for an upcoming shoot and arranging for production people and artists
- Making sure that the video will be completed within a given budget
- Managing people to make sure that everyone is there and ready to work
- Deciding on a venue for the video, either in a studio or in a real-world setting
- Setting up backgrounds and props, if needed
- Deciding on the "look" or style that should be achieved by the video
- Transporting and setting up equipment

Creating a good music video means creating a fun and engaging advertisement for the musician or band, both showcasing their musical performance and providing an entertaining film clip.

Editing raw video footage into a professional finished video takes time and skill. It also involves the artistic talent to create the mood or feeling that the video is meant to convey.

- Spending twelve-hour days producing the actual video footage
- Editing footage to create the actual video

PREPARING YOURSELF

So what can you do to prepare for a career making music videos? Some people working in the field do have four-year college degrees in areas such as arts management or film and video. But the most important way to find an "in" to the field is by starting as an intern in a music production company, working up to an assistant producer, and eventually becoming a producer. "It's an easier route to get paid," said Amy E. on CFNC.org. "And you can get some set work by working in the office. Any time someone goes out to shoot, you can go with them, and then you move into the role of producer eventually." On-the-job training is the best way into the field. Another good way to prepare is to make your own videos for friends who have bands, both to develop skills and build a portfolio of your work.

FROM SKATEBOARD VIDEOS TO MUSIC VIDEOS

Adam Powell directs music videos for many of the top musical artists in England. But he got his start shooting home videos of his friends at a local skate park. Because of the skate videos, Powell got very interested in making videos, which eventually led to music videos: "While I was at university, I was still making skate videos... My friend's band had just signed to Metal Blade Records. They liked my skate videos, and approached me to make a video for their song 'Only Tools and Corpses.' At the time I had no intention of making music videos, but I just went for it." He created a video using zombies with hammers, casting friends and improvising makeup. At the time, MySpace was becoming popular and provided a good audience for music videos, so Powell offered to make videos for many bands he liked. Eventually, he was employed by a production company and has worked his way up to directing videos for well-known bands. His advice to aspiring video producers? "If I was starting now I'd approach everything in the same way; I'd put my heart into it. You have to be true in what you're doing and true to yourself, and don't put formats and technology before 'soul.' One piece of advice that I always give people is: don't try and make what you think a music video should be, make what you feel is right."

Music video production may include filming a musical group during live concert events, which can be challenging because of the crowds, poor lighting, and special effects.

Ultimately you can assemble a reel of sample videos to show potential employers. It also helps to closely study existing music videos. Starting in high school, it would be helpful to take any film or video production classes that your school offers, as well as volunteering to make videos of school events. This also provides experience in managing people and locations.

FUTURE PROSPECTS

There is no avoiding the fact that the industry of music video production is struggling a little right now. This is partly due to the fact that the music industry itself is struggling because of issues like illegal music downloads, and there isn't as much money available for making videos. Television channels are also playing fewer videos. But they are a form of advertising for musicians, and advertising will always be needed in the music industry. Some experts see music videos gaining in popularity again in the coming years. The US Bureau of Labor Statistics estimates that the field will grow more slowly than most occupations, at only about 3 percent over the next five years. But video production careers do pay better than many other careers, and there is the creative satisfaction of making videos.

FOR MORE INFORMATION

BOOKS

Atinsky, Steve, and Dena Seif. *LA 411: The Professional Reference Guide for Film, Television, Commercial and Music Video Production*. New York, NY: 411 Publishing, 2008.
A directory of resources for the video production industry.

Lusted, Marcia Amidon. *Inside the Industry: Entertainment*. Minneapolis, MN: Abdo, 2011.
A look at the various careers available in the entertainment industry, including music production.

Manriquez, Antonio, and Tom McCluskey. *Video Production 101: Delivering the Message*. San Francisco, CA: Peachpit Press, 2014.
This book explores the roles of story development, production, direction, camera work, editing, sound design, and other important aspects of media creation.

Owsinski, Bobby. *The Musician's Video Handbook*. Milwaukee, WI: Hal Leonard, 2010.
This book describes everything a musician needs to know to easily make any of the various types of videos that are now required of a musical artist for promotion.

ORGANIZATIONS

Association of Music Producers
3 West 18th Street, 5th floor
New York, NY 10011
(212) 924-4100
Website: http://www.ampnow.com
The Association of Music Producers (AMP) was
  founded in 1998 to educate its members, as well
  as the larger production, advertising, and media
  communities, on all facets of music production,
  from creation to final use.

National Association of Record Industry Professionals
PO Box 2446
Toluca Lake, CA 91610-2446
Website: http://www.narip.com
This organization brings professionals from the
  music industry together, offering career services
  and support.

PERIODICALS

Videomaker
645 Mangrove Avenue
Chico, CA 95926-3946

(530) 891-8410

Website: http://www.videomaker.com

Videomaker is a magazine for people who use video as a common way to communicate. It includes industry news, product reviews, and tips and techniques for making better videos.

BLOGS

Epik Music Videos

Website: http://www.epikmusicvideos.com/blog.html

A behind-the-scenes blog from one of London's best music video production companies.

WEBSITES

Because of the changing nature of internet links, Rosen Publishing has developed an online list of websites related to the subject of this book. This site is updated regularly. Please use this link to access this list:

http://www.rosen links.com/CCWC/camera

CHAPTER 5

CINEMA PROJECTIONIST

There's one person who works at a movie theater who doesn't get a lot of attention. But without him or her, there would be no movie viewing taking place at all. This person is the projectionist, the one responsible for making sure that those big canisters of movie film make it onto the screen. It's a great career for people who love cameras and working with film, as well as those who love to watch lots of movies as part of their job.

In an older movie theater, a projectionist may run several mechanical projectors at once in different rooms. In modern theaters, the work is less physical and digital projection systems are being used instead of mechanical projectors and film reels. The use of digital systems is expected to limit the opportunities for projectionists as the function becomes more auto-mated, but the equipment used by different theaters will vary widely.

For people who love watching movies, the job of movie projectionist may seem more like play than work. They are basically paid to watch movies all the time!

Running a traditional mechanical projector with film is a complicated task. A motion picture projectionist is responsible for the delivery and pickup of 35mm prints for the featured films at the theater. Once a film print is delivered, the projectionist will unspool the film and roll it on to a large plate. He or she must then thread the film through the movie house projector and connect it to a second reel, where the 35mm print will be rolled. Each print usually comes with two to three separate spools that must be spliced together on a film splicer. In a single screen theater, a projectionist works from a second-story room with a small window from which to project the film. He or she makes certain the film is in focus and synchronized to the sound.

Some movies require even more technical work, such as 3D movies, for which projector lenses must be changed to make the 3D effect work.

Some projectionists work at film festivals, such as the famous Venice Film Festival in Italy, where they show the films that are competing for prestigious awards.

Even new digital projectors need to be attended to since the equipment is sensitive. A projectionist must be able to fix anything that doesn't work before it becomes a problem and so that it doesn't interrupt a movie showing.

Cinema projectionists don't just work in movie theaters. They may also work at drive-in movie theaters, film festivals, schools and colleges, and even at corporate meetings or trade shows and conferences. Even if they are working at a location with its own setup for audio-visual presentations, a projectionist has to be able to figure out how to make that equipment work.

A DAY IN THE LIFE OF A CINEMA PROJECTIONIST

What daily tasks are part of working as a cinema projectionist? Most projectionists are employed by movie theaters, although a few may own a small theater and carry out projection duties rather than paying a dedicated projectionist. Tasks include:

- Receiving and checking the film reels
- Loading the films onto the projector in the right order
- Making sure that the film runs smoothly through the projector and checking that sound is operating properly
- Joining ("splicing") lengths of film together if they break
- Storing the films safely

In large cities such as New York, with hundreds of movie theaters, projectionists may have an easier time finding jobs since there are more opportunities.

- Sending on the reels to other theaters when a run of a movie is completed
- Looking after the projection equipment, either repairing it or calling for service if necessary
- Being responsible for heating, lighting, ventilation, and alarm systems in the cinema
- For digital screening, coordinating online delivery of the films with the distributor and managing the security systems for allowing the films to be screened

Showing movies at a film festival or other location might also involve dealing with many different film types and projectors. This is why a projectionist needs good mechanical and technical skills and a knowledge of computers. Most projectionists also work from early afternoon until late at night, depending on the movie showing times.

PREPARING YOURSELF

Projectionists generally do not need a college education. They do need to be eighteen years of age in order to be able to watch adult films. It is helpful to have video and audio experience and a mechanical or technical aptitude, but most of the job skills will be learned during on-the-job training. Computer skills will be increasingly important as more theaters move to digital projection. Most theaters are owned by large companies that have comprehensive training programs for their employees and may also cross-train them in other areas of theater work, such as the ticket counter or concession stand, in case they should be needed there.

Anyone interested in a career working in a movie theater should take audio and visual tech classes in high school, as well as study film history and stay current with new films.

FUTURE PROSPECTS

The outlook for cinema projectionists is uncertain due to changing technology and the move from film to digital as the media for showing movies. The US Bureau of Labor Statistics estimates that the job growth will actually be negative because of this. However, the technical skills for the job are also useful in other fields, and a cinema projectionist who is willing to learn the skills for digital movie projection will continue to have employment in movie theaters.

FOR MORE INFORMATION

BOOKS

Corrigan, Timothy. *The Film Experience: An Introduction*, 4th ed. New York, NY: St. Martin's Press, 2014.
An introduction to studying films and their history.

Levy, Frederick. *Hollywood 101: The Film Industry*. Los Angeles, CA: Renaissance Books, 2000.
A behind-the-scenes guide to jobs in the cinema industry and how to get them.

Nichols, Bill. *Engaging Cinema: An Introduction to Film Studies*. New York, NY: W. W. Norton, 2010.
A beginning guide to the area of film studies.

Saetervadet, Torkell. *The Advanced Projection Manual*. New York, NY: FIAF, 2006.
A technical manual for projectionists, especially in regards to the transition to digital movie media.

Saetervadet, Torkell. *FIAF Digital Projection Guide*. New York, NY: FIAF, 2012.
A technical guide to digital film projection.

ORGANIZATIONS

Giant Screen Cinema Association
624 Holly Springs Road, Suite 243
Holly Springs, NC 27540

(919) 346-1123

Website: http://www.giantscreencinema.com

Organization of filmmakers, distributors, theaters, suppliers, manufacturers, and students that promotes unity in the cinema industry.

International Cinema Technology Association

825 8th Avenue 29th Floor

New York, NY 10019

(212) 493-4097

Website: http:// www.internationalcinematechnologyassociation.com

This organization promotes technological advances in the global theater market.

National Association of Theatre Owners

1705 N. Street NW

Washington, DC 20036

(202) 962-0054

Website: http://www.natoonline.org

This organization unites theater owners from all fifty states and over 32,000 screens.

PERIODICALS

Variety
11175 Santa Monica Boulevard
Los Angeles, CA 90025
(323) 617-9100
Website: http://variety.com
Variety is the magazine for the entertainment industry,
    including movies and television.

WEBSITES

Because of the changing nature of internet links, Rosen
Publishing has developed an online list of websites
related to the subject of this book. This site is updated
regularly. Please use this link to access this list:

http://www.rosenlinks.com/CCWC/camera

CHAPTER 6

DIGITAL FILM COLORIST

For people who love to watch movies, love to experiment with computers, and have a good eye for color and the elements of a good photo, then the job of a digital colorist can combine all of these things. Digital colorist is a job that has been created by the use of digital moviemaking. During the final editing of a movie, colorists correct the colors in scenes, brightening anything that looks bland or boring. They also touch up the appearance of actors so that their skin, hair, and clothing look flawless. They can cover up under-eye shadows or blemishes and even out skin tones. Their work on actors is so important to their image that many actors now write digital coloring into their contracts to make sure it is done. With a sharp eye for every aspect of a movie's scenes, the digital colorist makes movies look brighter, more appealing, and more exciting. It can be as simple as enhancing the colors of a sunset to make it more vivid, or more complicated, such as making a new vehicle look old and worn. They also make sure that every shot matches the shots before and after so the movie looks seamless.

A digital colorist needs to make sure that the colors in a movie are vivid, accurate, and consistent. Many actors rely on colorists to make them look as good as possible on screen.

To be successful, digital colorists need to have specific traits. They need to be flexible and to work well with other people since the final edit of a movie and its final look are a collaborative process between the director and the post-production staff, especially the director of photography. Colorists need a good eye for detail, as well as a love for movies and good observation skills. Since their job is to correct anything in the movie that does not look good, they have to scrutinize every frame and every scene for possible flaws. And all of this might have to be done quickly, under a deadline for finishing the movie before its release date.

Digital colorists usually work in movie studios or offices, and their working hours may be long and irregular when they are under pressure to finish a movie. They may have a great deal of work at one time and then have a dry spell of unemployment during which they have no work at all until they are signed on to a new project.

A DAY IN THE LIFE OF A DIGITAL COLORIST

A colorist's day depends on where he or she is in the movie-making process. Some tasks must be done before work begins and others during and after a movie is completely edited. Tasks include:

- Working with the director and director of photography to discuss the look that they want for the movie
- Interpreting the ideas of the directors and other postproduction staff
- Watching the movie closely and observing places where coloring needs to be corrected or enhanced
- Observing actors closely in the movie and seeing where their appearances need to be enhanced or corrected

PLEASANTVILLE

Unlike most movies, *Pleasantville*, which takes place partly within a black-and-white vintage television show, required that color correction be done in reverse, to make certain scenes filmed in color look like they were actually black and white.

In 1998, the director and cinematographer for the New Line Cinema movie *Pleasantville* actually worked the color correction process in reverse. Because *Pleasantville's* story line deals with black and white and color as part of the plot, the entire movie was shot in color. Then they had to remove the color (a process called desaturation) from the parts of the movie that needed to appear to be black and white. This ended up being a joint process of the colorists and the special effects department.

- Making sure the look of the movie and the scenery shots are consistent
- Using different technologies to make color corrections to the film
- Offering solutions to problems in the film, either color related or having to do with special effects
- Keeping accurate records and notes of the process
- Making sure all editing work on the film is backed up and saved

PREPARING YOURSELF

Some digital colorists have college degrees in film production, but many of them learn on the job. Any courses in film study, video production, and film production that are available in high school will be helpful, as well as art courses that deal in photography and color. For students who don't want to earn a college degree, it is best to find employment in the film industry, perhaps as an apprentice or assistant in the postproduction department, and then learn and progress through watching and training with established colorists. It also helps to be familiar with computer programs, the telecine process for transferring motion picture film into video, and the digital intermediate (DI) process for digitizing a motion picture and manipulating the color and other image characteristics.

The 1939 movie *The Wizard of Oz* required that some parts of the movie be in black and white and others be in color.

FUTURE PROSPECTS

Like many other careers in digital filmmaking, especially film and video editors, the job of digital colorists is expected to grow about 11 percent over the next ten years, faster than many professions. It is also a highly competitive career since it pays well and has the added appeal of being part of the movie industry. The best places for digital colorists are New York City and Los Angeles, with their film and television industries.

FOR MORE INFORMATION

BOOKS

Hullfish, Steve. *The Art and Technique of Digital Color Correction*, 2nd ed. Waltham, MA: Focal Press, 2012.
A guide to the basics of color correction, often used as a textbook in film classes.

Hullfish, Steve, and Jaime Fowler. *Color Correction for Video: Using Desktop Tools to Perfect Your Image*, 2nd ed. Waltham, MA: Focal Press, 2008.
Tips, tools, and techniques for enhancing videos on a home computer.

Hurkman, Alexis van. *Color Correction Handbook: Professional Techniques for Video and Cinema*, 2nd ed. San Francisco, CA: Peachpit Press, 2013.
The standard guide for learning the processes of color correction.

Hurkman, Alexis van. *Color Correction Look Book: Creative Grading Techniques for Film and Video*. San Francisco, CA: Peachpit Press, 2013.
A handbook for grading and stylizing film with color correction.

ORGANIZATIONS

American Cinema Editors
100 Universal City Plaza, Building 9128, Suite 260
Universal City, CA 91608
(818) 777-2900
Website: https://americancinemaeditors.org
The official society of motion picture editors, founded in
1950. Membership is based on accomplishments, but
it has a student editing competition.

Motion Picture Editors Guild
7715 Sunset Boulevard
Suite 200
Hollywood, CA 90046
(323) 876-4770
Website: http://www.editorsguild.com/?source
=filmmakers.com
A labor union that represents all postproduction
professionals in the motion picture industry,
protecting their interests and ensuring the highest
level of achievement in the field.

PERIODICALS

Cinema Editor
100 Universal City Plaza
Building 9128, Room 260
Universal City, CA 91608
(818) 777-2900
Website: http://www.cinemaeditormagazine.com
This magazine is for film and television editors and
assistants, as well as postproduction experts in
these fields. It includes articles about editing and
recent movies, tips, and behind-the-scenes looks at
film editing.

Editor's Guild
7715 Sunset Boulevard, Suite 200
Hollywood, CA 90046
(800) 705-8700
Website: http://www.editorsguild.com/v2/magazine
/archives/0707/features_article04.htm

WEBSITES

Because of the changing nature of internet links, Rosen Publishing has developed an online list of websites related to the subject of this book. This site is updated regularly. Please use this link to access this list:

http://www.rosenlinks.com/CCWC/camera

CHAPTER 7

MOVIE KEY GRIP

If you've ever paid close attention to the credits that run after a movie, you've probably wondered exactly what a grip was. If you like simply to be around cameras and the moviemaking process and don't necessarily have to be the one taking the shots or filming, it could be a good career to learn more about. A grip is a member of the team that is responsible for building and maintaining the equipment that is used for supporting the cameras, as well as moving and setting up that equipment. A key grip is the supervisor of the team of grips. Not only is it a position that is directly involved in how cameras are used in moviemaking, it's also a common entry into other moviemaking jobs. In any movie, especially during action sequences, there are many camera angles and special shots, from the air, forward and back, and left and right. All those different angles and perspectives make the movie much more interesting and exciting. And they can happen only because of the work of a grip. Key grips are responsible for the whole process

A key grip helps create and rig the equipment needed for using cameras during moviemaking. They are especially important for taking shots with unusual or difficult camera angles.

One job of the key grip is to build tracks and dollies for moving camera shots. These pieces of equipment allow cameras to move smoothly and easily during filming.

of rigging and placing the camera equipment. Their job is a combination of carpenter, mechanic, electrician, and rigger, and they are part of the essential people who make movies happen but aren't the "upfront" people, like directors and actors. Their work can be fun. As Job Monkey puts it:

> There is no other job where you will have to put a camera inside a tomato cart, strap a camera to a strut of a buzzing helicopter, or use a light to brighten a roulette table. Key grips get paid for creative manual labor, plus they get their names lost in the credits of every production.

Key grips don't just work in the movie industry. They also work in television, as well as places like concert halls and event venues like auditoriums and stadiums, where frequent performances require different equipment. Sometimes they are employed on the road crew of a traveling production, band, or musician. They might build the track needed to run a camera on a dolly to film a marathon. Or perhaps there's a scene in a television show where a camera needs to be in a tree, and the grips build scaffolding for that. They might also create scaffolds or move lighting to certain places to achieve a particular effect, like a certain kind of shadow. They will work anywhere that filming takes place, in the United States or other countries.

Key grips' work pattern is basically one of "hurry up and wait," meaning that they might spend hours sitting around waiting for filming to begin and then suddenly have to scramble to set up equipment in a particular way. They may suddenly have to position cranes, tracks, dollies, microphones, and lighting as quickly as possible.

A DAY IN THE LIFE OF A KEY GRIP

A key grip spends his or her day in calm or in chaos, depending on the circumstances. But many of the following tasks take place:

- Checking in with the cinematographer and the director of photography to see what they require
- Directing grips to load or unload equipment needed and set it up

MANY GRIPS, MANY JOBS

There is more than one kind of grip on a movie set. The key grip is the one who supervises all the grips. But there are also specific jobs that certain grips do. Dolly grips work with camera dollies, which are small carts with wheels that run on tracks, with the camera mounted on them on a platform. Construction grips specialize in building the platforms and sets needed for certain camera angles. A best boy grip (and these can be either men or women) is a little bit like a traffic controller. He or she determines how many grips are needed on a set and is ultimately responsible for making sure that the right equipment is at the right location.

- Working with the chief lighting technician (called a gaffer) to map and plan the lighting and camera placement for every scene
- Problem solving during filming to achieve a particular effect or solve a problem
- Creating special equipment to hold a camera for difficult or unusual shots
- Securing cameras during all types of shots so that the filming is smooth and the camera is protected
- Packing, loading, and transporting all equipment at the end of the day

One easy way to prepare for working as a grip is to experiment with camera angles and unusual shots by taking videos with a smartphone.

PREPARING YOURSELF

Becoming a key grip does not require any special education or certification, although some grips do attend film school. Instead, it relies heavily on experience, as well as being good at skills like carpentry, electricity, problem solving, and rigging. Key grips also need to be physically fit and agile and not afraid of heights. The best way to become a key grip is first to be hired on as a grip on a crew. On-the-job training teaches grips the skills they need to know, and with enough experience and a good attitude, a grip can become a key grip and perhaps even move into more direct camera positions.

FUTURE PROSPECTS

According to the US Department of Labor, the job outlook for jobs in the video and film industry, including camera operators, is expected to increase faster than the average for all jobs. Now that people are creating video content for new devices, such as tablets and smartphones, the prospects for anyone working in the filmmaking industries is good. Key grips are also unlikely to be displaced by automation since their job is very mechanical and physical and can't be accomplished by computers and digital effects alone.

FOR MORE INFORMATION

BOOKS

Bill, Tony. *Movie Speak: How to Talk Like You Belong on a Film Set*. New York, NY: Workman Publishing, 2009.
A guide to the unusual and specialized vocabulary and slang terms that are used on a movie set.

Box, Harry. *Set Lighting Technician's Handbook: Film Lighting Equipment, Practice, and Electrical Distribution*, 4th ed. Waltham, MA: Focal Press, 2010.
A good manual for anyone involved in motion picture lighting.

Elkins, David E. *The Camera Assistant's Manual*, 6th ed. Waltham, MA: Focal Press, 2013.
This book explains how to be an assistant cameraman, including what to do—and what not to do—on the job.

Uva, Michael G. *The Grip Book: The Studio Grip's Essential Guide*, 5th ed. Waltham, MA: Focal Press, 2013.
An essential guide to the skills needed for becoming a professional movie grip.

ORGANIZATIONS

American Society of Cinematographers
PO Box 2230
Los Angeles, CA 90028
(800) 448-0145
Website: http://www.theasc.com/site
This organization advances the art and science of
cinematography and brings people together to
discuss their work.

International Alliance of Theatrical Stage Employees
IATSE General Office
207 W. 25th Street, 4th floor
New York, NY 10001
(212) 730-1770
Website: http://iatse.net
This labor union represents virtually all the
behind- the-scenes workers in movie, theater, and
television, ranging from motion picture animator to
theater usher.

PERIODICALS

MovieMaker
2525 Michigan Avenue, Building i
Santa Monica, CA 90404
(310) 828-8388
Website: http://www.moviemaker.com
This is the industry's most widely read resource on the
   art and business of making movies, as well as the
   independent film industry. It includes interviews, tips,
   behind-the-scenes looks, and coverage of festivals.

APPS

Gobo (Filmmakers Dictionary) by Agent 49 (iTunes).
   Knowing the meanings of the terms and slang
   commonly used on a production is an invaluable
   tool for anyone working in or aspiring to work in the
   entertainment industry. The Filmmakers Dictionary
   app not only features a glossary of industry words
   and phrases but also defines vocabulary used within
   different departments.

The Grip App by Enlightened Shenanigans (iTunes).
   Created by grips and electric department
   professionals, the educational and instructional app

is a useful reference tool for aspiring grips. Featuring an array of equipment images and a dictionary of grip terms, the app also provides equipment specifications, how-to guides, and step-by-step instructions to teach users about dollies, cranes, hardware, and rigs.

iHandy Carpenter By iHandy Inc. (Google Play) (iTunes). The carpenter tool kit app features five handy tools, including a plumb bob, a surface level, a bubble level bar, a protractor, and a ruler. In addition to measuring angels up to 180 degrees, you can calibrate the plumb bob, surface level, and level bar so the app can be used as an inclinometer/clinometer. The ruler can measure either in inches or centimeters and can determine the length of objects longer than your smartphone.

WEBSITES

Because of the changing nature of internet links, Rosen Publishing has developed an online list of websites related to the subject of this book. This site is updated regularly. Please use this link to access this list:

http://www.rosenlinks.com/CCWC/camera

CHAPTER 8

TELESCOPE OPERATOR TECHNICIAN

If you are interested in cameras, and especially in lenses and perspective, then the job of a telescope operator technician may be right for you, and it's probably something you've never heard of. It's even better if you love the night sky and are fascinated by stargazing. These technicians aren't astronomers. Instead, they are more like engineers whose responsibility is the daily operations and maintenance of large telescopes and the other visual equipment that is part of a large observatory. Astronomers who search the skies for quasars, nebulae, stars, and even other galaxies couldn't do it without telescope operator techs who make sure that the telescopes and other equipment are in good working order and

Giant telescopes are sensitive and require constant care and adjustments to work well, which is the job of a telescope operator technician. They make the work of astronomers possible.

that the telescopes are aligned to the part of the sky that the astronomer wants to study.

The giant telescopes that astronomers use in observatories are sensitive instruments that need constant care and adjusting. Even though a telescope operator tech works at night, when almost all telescopes are used, he or she has to arrive around sunset to help the telescope adjust from warm daytime temperatures inside the observatory to cooler outside night temperatures. The operator also has to learn how these giant telescopes work, with their magnifying lenses, large glass reflecting plates, and gears. Mechanical ability is important, as well as good math skills, to learn the coordinate system and the language that astronomers use to label and describe sections of the sky.

A DAY IN THE LIFE OF A TELESCOPE OPERATOR TECHNICIAN

While the duties of a telescope operator technician may vary depending on the type of telescope and the organization of the observatory, there are tasks common to all telescopes:

- Operation and monitoring of the telescope and support equipment
- Monitoring system alarm signals and error messages
- Detecting, analyzing, diagnosing, and resolving problems

The Hubble Telescope is one of the most famous telescopes used to observe deep space. Unlike observatory telescopes, it takes photos from a low orbit around Earth.

SEEING STARS

Michael Alegria is not an astronomer, but he loves the night sky. And he is one of just a few people who know how to operate the Multiple Mirror Telescope (MMT) in Amado, Arizona. "I make sure the telescope is pointed where it's supposed to be pointed, what the instrument is doing, what it's supposed to be doing and everything else associated with that," Alegria said in an interview with National Public Radio. He is a telescope operator technician, and his job begins with using a hand winch to roll up the shade that covers the telescope and then opening the large observatory doors. While the telescope mirrors cool to the same temperature as the outside air, he moves to the control room, where he will spend the night. He monitors a bank of computer and video displays. Michael Hart, an astronomer who works with Alegria, said of him, "Mike is my hero. Mike makes the whole telescope operate single-handedly," Hart says. "We would not be here conducting these experiments if Mike were not here to support us." The MMT has made some great discoveries, including the presence of water on the moon, and Alegria is part of that. He especially likes witnessing the discoveries.

Telescope operator techs make sure that observatory telescopes, like this one, are adjusted between day and night temperatures and ready to observe the night sky.

- Collecting weather, environmental, and system data
- Keeping a log of events and data for every shift
- Maintaining safety and security of the facility
- Transporting observers to and from the observatory
- Setup and shutdown of the telescope and instruments
- Operation of instruments
- Troubleshooting of instruments
- Taking of observational data
- Data reduction (translating data into a simplified and corrected form)

Not all operator techs will do data reduction, and some may conduct tours and outreach programs for visitors. It depends on the type of observatory and how many people staff it.

PREPARING YOURSELF

Becoming a telescope operator technician does not require a college degree, but many operators may earn a certificate as an optical lenses technician, which requires several years of education. Most techs learn on the job, from other technicians or even from astronomers at the observatory. The best techs have an aptitude for good time management and attention to detail, and mechanical aptitude and familiarity with computers is also helpful. Some telescope operator techs may decide to attend college to gain the skills necessary to become astronomers.

FUTURE PROSPECTS

The job outlook for people working in astronomy and related jobs is not expected to grow as fast as other occupations. This is partly because observatories are often linked to government projects, and there isn't currently as much funding for these programs. However, colleges and universities will continue to support observatories and astronomy programs, so technicians will still be needed to make these telescopes function.

FOR MORE INFORMATION

BOOKS

Jefferis, David. *Star Spotters: Telescopes and Observatories*. New York, NY: Crabtree Publishing, 2009.
This book answers questions about telescopes, observatories, and astronomy.

McCray, W. Patrick. *Giant Telescopes: Astronomical Ambition and the Promise of Technology*. Cambridge, MA: Harvard University Press, 2006.
This book tells about the history, planning, and construction of modern telescopes.

Petersen, Carolyn Collins. *Astronomy 101: From the Sun and Moon to Wormholes and Warp Drive, Key Theories, Discoveries, and Facts about the Universe*. New York, NY: Adams Media, 2013.
This book provides basic facts about astronomy and space but also has many fascinating facts, charts, and images to answer questions about the universe.

ORGANIZATIONS

American Astronomical Society

2000 Florida Avenue NW, Suite 300
Washington, DC 20009-1231
(202) 328-2010
Website: https://www.aas.org
AAS is the major association of professional
    astronomers in the United States. Its mission is
    to enhance and share human understanding of
    the universe.

National Space Science & Technology Institute
PO Box 49444
Colorado Springs, CO 80949-9444
Website: http://www.nssti.org/home.aspx
NSSTI's mission is to enlighten, inspire, and engage
    students, teachers, professionals, and the public
    in the adventure and possibilities of space science
    and technology.

PERIODICALS

Astronomy
PO Box 1612
Waukesha, WI 53187

Website: http://www.astronomy.com
Includes stories about astronomical events,
    conferences, people in the astronomy world,
    equipment reviews, and amazing photographs.

Sky & Telescope
PO Box 420235
Palm Coast, FL 32142-0235
(888) 253-0230
Website: http://www.skyandtelescope.com
Intended for amateur astronomers, this magazine
    contains information about recent discoveries,
    telescopes and other equipment, and astronomical
    events, as well as resources and education
    in astronomy.

VIDEOS

"The Great Refractor Telescope at Lick Observatory,
    Mount Hamilton; California"
https://www.youtube.com/watch?v=0DZsQW2Op8Q

BLOGS

Large Binocular Telescope Observatory News
https://www.mmto.org/blog

This blog contains news and information from the LBTO
in Arizona.

MMT Observatory
https://www.mmto.org/blog
This blog shares events, discoveries, and other
astronomy-related information from the MMT
in Arizona.

WEBSITES

Because of the changing nature of internet links, Rosen
Publishing has developed an online list of websites
related to the subject of this book. This site is updated
regularly. Please use this link to access this list:

http://www.rosenlinks.com/CCWC/camera

CHAPTER 9

FORENSIC (CRIME SCENE) PHOTOGRAPHER

Almost every crime drama on television or in the movies seems to have a scene where a crime is committed and the police photographer is busy taking photos of the area where the crime took place. This isn't just a Hollywood thing. These photographers, called crime scene or forensic photographers, are an important part of any crime scene investigation. Their job is to document everything at a crime scene or an accident, both to make a record of it and as possible evidence in a court case. They photograph everything, from bullet holes and tire tracks to fingerprints, footprints, and even blood splatters and the position of any dead bodies. They create a permanent visual record of the

The job of a forensic photographer can involve arriving on the scene before the police and photographing weapons used in committing crimes.

crime or accident scene, which can be referred to long after the actual scene has been cleaned up.

Being a forensic photographer is not for everyone, as some may be easily upset by gruesome scenes. It can be emotionally difficult to photograph both deceased people and living people who have been badly injured in an accident or assault. Photographers also have to work in these environments without disturbing any critical evidence or interfering with the rest of the investigative team.

Most forensic photographers are employed directly by the police or a company that specializes in forensics services. They may also be employed by insurance companies or lawyers, who need detailed information about accident scenes in order to process insurance claims or determine guilt in a court case. Forensic photographers usually arrive on the scene of a crime or accident as quickly as possible, even before police in some cases, to take photos before anything is moved or changed. They also use their judgment to decide what is important to photograph since a small detail could turn out to be incredibly important later in an investigation. They also organize their shots in the same order as the criminal events took place, if possible, so that there is context and a record of the timeline of the crime. They also take multiple shots from many different angles and perspectives so that viewers can understand the scene as completely as possible just through looking at photographs. They may also mark items in a photograph with flags or numbered plastic markers to make certain types of evidence show up better in photographs and give perspective as to their size.

REALITY VERSUS TELEVISION

TV shows like *CSI*, where forensic investigators deal with crime scenes, have become very popular. But how realistic are they? Most forensics experts say that there are a few elements of reality, but a lot of things aren't true to life. For example, on television, with its hour-long format, investigations and the results of them happen at a much faster pace than in real life. TV forensic investigators have the latest technology, which, in reality, many police departments can't afford. As Stefanie Elliott, a crime scene technician in Florida, said, "On '*CSI*,' they manage to get perfect fingerprints off everything. But suspects rarely leave clear or complete fingerprints because they only touch things very, very, very briefly." She continued, "Fingerprints are very useful, but they are not as prevalent as '*CSI*' would have you believe. In addition, since evidence is sent to labs to be analyzed, it often takes months to get results because labs are backlogged. On television, investigators get results almost instantly. But right now, the state crime lab is 995 cases behind on DNA."

A DAY IN THE LIFE OF A FORENSIC PHOTOGRAPHER

Being a forensic photographer requires a combination of skills. They must be part police officer, part photographer. Most forensic photographers are on call for specific shifts during the week, which means they may be called to a crime scene at 2:00 AM. Some of the basic tasks of a forensic photographer include:

- Setting up the site for the shoot
- Selecting proper film type, camera, camera settings, exposure, and angles
- Monitoring and maintaining photographic supplies
- Video recording crime scenes, as necessary
- Using the best equipment and techniques for each environment and lighting condition

Numbered plastic markers help make sure that certain types of evidence show up well in photographs. They also add size perspective, so that those viewing the photographs know how big the objects were.

Like many things in television and movies, the job of a forensic photographer as seen on film is often not a very realistic portrayal of the real thing.

- Capturing images that have maximum depth of field, are free from distortion, and are in sharp focus
- Following proper police methods
- Keeping detailed records of the location the image was taken, the type of camera and lens used, and whether flash or artificial lights were used

PREPARING YOURSELF

Forensic photography is a field where you can get started with only a high school diploma, but to really progress in the field, it will at some point be necessary to get a college degree or a certificate. Many forensic photographers start out as police officers since they will already have a grounding in police procedure and criminal investigations. Taking courses in photography as well as criminal justice (some high schools offer vocational classes like these) will help provide a head start. Initial employment may be as an assistant to an established photographer, and there are also opportunities for internships while in high school. Without police training, most of the procedural knowledge will be learned on the job. Ultimately, it's important to attend college and get a degree in photography or criminal justice. There is also a professional certificate in forensic photography, which combines classroom time with experience in the field. The Federal Bureau of Investigation (FBI) offers this training, as well as local and state law enforcement organizations. Once a photographer earns a forensic photography certificate, he or she is eligible for more jobs and will earn a higher salary.

FUTURE PROSPECTS

The job outlook is good for anyone working in the forensic science occupations, including forensic photographers. The field is expected to grow by 27 percent in the coming decade, much faster than other occupations. However, because it is a small, specialized field, jobs will still be very competitive. With this in mind, it's best to plan on getting a degree or a certification in forensic photography at some point, to be more appealing to future employers.

FOR MORE INFORMATION

BOOKS

Duncan, Christopher D. *Advanced Crime Scene Photography*, 2nd ed. Boca Raton, FL: CRC Press, 2015.
This book details how to collect photographic evidence for investigations and court cases, especially in environments that aren't especially camera friendly.

Gardner, Ross M. *Practical Crime Scene Processing and Investigation*, 2nd ed. Boca Raton, FL: CRC Press, 2011.
This book gives the basics of crime scene processing and proper procedures.

Robinson, Edward M. *Crime Scene Photography*, 3rd ed. Cambridge, MA: Academic Press, 2016.
An introduction to the basic concepts of forensic photography.

Robinson, Edward M. *Introduction to Crime Scene Photography*. Cambridge, MA: Academic Press, 2012.
This book presents the essentials of basic crime scene photography techniques.

Staggs, Steven. *Crime Scene and Evidence Photography*. Wildomar, CA: Staggs Publishing, 2014.
Intended for all law enforcement personnel, this book provides instructions for photographing different types of crime scenes and evidence.

ORGANIZATIONS

American Academy of Forensic Sciences
410 North 21st Street
Colorado Springs, CO 80904
(719) 636-1100
Website: http://www.aafs.org
AAFS is dedicated to the application of science
to law enforcement. Its members include all
the different professions of forensic science,
including photographers.

Evidence Photographers International Council (EPIC)
229 Peachtree Street NE, #2200
Atlanta, GA 30303
(866) 868-EPIC (3742)
Website: http://www.evidencephotographers.com
EPIC's mission is to provide members with education
and resources to aid in the advancement of
evidence photography.

BLOGS

Crime Scene Photography
http://crimescenephotography.blogspot.com
This blog includes tutorials and news about
photography of crime scenes and victims.

Forensic News
http://forensicnews.blogspot.com
This blog includes forensic news as well as explanations of misconceptions about crime scene investigations.

WEBSITES

Because of the changing nature of internet links, Rosen Publishing has developed an online list of websites related to the subject of this book. This site is updated regularly. Please use this link to access this list:

http://www.rosenlinks.com/CCWC/camera

Of all the many types of photography careers, one that receives little attention is that of a scientific photographer. Scientific photographers may not have glamorous careers or become household names, but they have another, more important purpose. The photographs they take, which are usually for scientific research, medicine, astronomy, and forensics, may help with the discovery of a new medical treatment or an unknown galaxy. Scientific photographers mostly work in research facilities, government

Scientific photographers may find themselves working in harsh or unusual locations, depending on the type of things they are photographing and where they are found.

FELICE FRANKEL

Felice Frankel has made a career out of science photography. For twenty years, she has worked with scientists at MIT and Harvard University to document their scientific discoveries. Along the way, she has created ways to make these scientific photos more interesting to look at. Her images, which have included yeast colonies shaped like daisies, rainbow-colored quantum dots, and soft flexible electronics that can be tattooed onto the skin, are known for being compelling enough that people who see them become excited about the subjects. According to BetaBoston:

> In a hyperconnected world where a powerful image can trigger a viral response, researchers are realizing that one great photograph can draw considerably more attention to their new work. Frankel's goal is to capture scientifically honest photographs that, in her words, "frankly, makes you want to look at it."

Frankel has pioneered ways to make the old standard black-and-white photos more vibrant and interesting. She hopes that her work will inspire scientists to make their work accessible to curious nonscientists.

departments, or colleges and universities. But they may also find work in the military, businesses, and even the arts. It's a photographic career with many possibilities.

Basically, scientific photographers use cameras to capture subjects that might be too small, too far away, too fast, or simply too difficult to see with the naked eye. Scientific photographers have many specialized techniques for achieving photographs of these difficult subjects. For example, they might use photomicrography, which means taking photos using a camera that is connected to a microscope. Or they might use infrared photography to take photographs of objects in space by photographing the heat reflected by those objects. They also use ultraviolet and fluorescent photography. Scientific photographers might even take photos using a camera that's floating in space, while they themselves are on Earth!

Scientific photographers do need a variety of skills to succeed. They need to have a good working knowledge of photography, but also of science, especially physics and optics. They need to have good attention to detail and be able to work as part of a team. They also need to be adept at setting up shots as well as keeping good records. They may have to interpret or use precise calculations. Patience and creativity are also helpful.

A DAY IN THE LIFE OF A SCIENTIFIC PHOTOGRAPHER

Photographic work required throughout any given day or week may involve shooting bacteria under magnification, super-fine particle research in a lab, genome research data, hybrid fuel ingredients—the potential subject matter is extensive. Some underwater photography may even be needed. Your job is to capture whatever subject you are assigned in the expository, illustrative, or abstract manner that your client wants.

What kinds of specific tasks are involved in the daily work of a scientific photographer?

- Working camera to take pictures of subject material to illustrate or record scientific or medical data or phenomena
- Planning methods and procedures for photographing subject material and setup of required equipment
- Observing and arranging subject material to desired position
- Engaging in research to develop new photographic procedure, materials, and scientific data
- Setting up, mounting, or installing photographic equipment and cameras
- Removing exposed film and developing film using chemicals, touch-up tools, and equipment

Scientific photography may also be used as a tool to collect and analyze data from difficult locations, like this coral reef. It provides scientists with another method for studying their subject.

- Photographing subject material to illustrate or record scientific/medical data or phenomena, using knowledge of scientific procedures and photographic technology and techniques
- Reviewing sets of photographs to select the best work

PREPARING YOURSELF

Like many photographic specialties, you can get started in the field of scientific photography without a college degree, but to advance in the career, eventually it is necessary to get a degree in photography, science, or scientific photography. To start out, a good grounding in photography and camera equipment is important, as well as basic scientific knowledge. Courses in photography, photographic editing, physics, biology, and other sciences can be taken in high school. On-the-job training may include learning to use

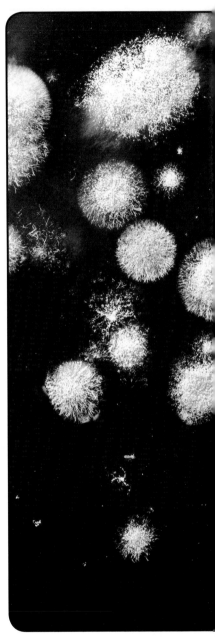

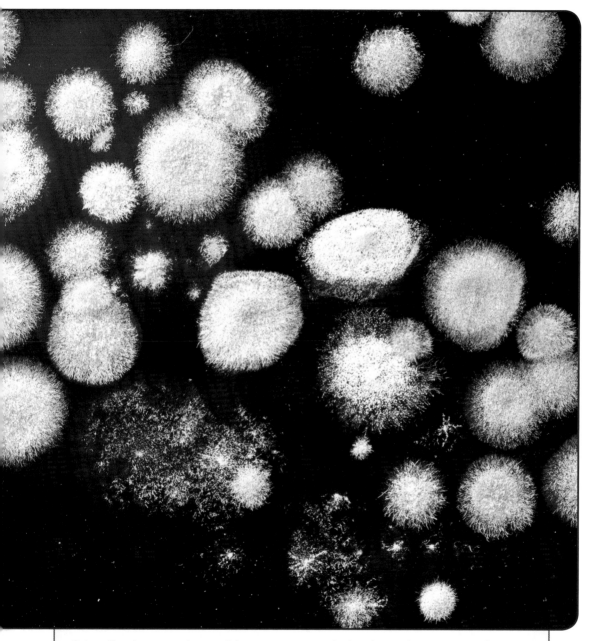

Scientific photography in a laboratory may include taking photographs of things like mold and bacteria and using photomicrography to capture images of extremely small things.

more sophisticated and specialized camera equipment. Some photographers start out as scientists and then learn photography to document and record their findings.

FUTURE PROSPECTS

The job outlook for scientific photographers is generally good and is expected to increase at about the average rate for all jobs. While scientific photographers are often salaried employees of the institutions or companies where they work, some work as freelancers. The trend is for more companies to use freelance photographers, which means that scientific photographers will have to compete for jobs and may not have a steady working income.

FOR MORE INFORMATION

BOOKS

Hubbell, Gerald. *Scientific Astrophotography: How Amateurs Can Generate and Use Professional Imaging Data*. New York, NY: Springer, 2012.
An amateur's guide to taking professional-quality photographs of space.

Matsumoto, Brian. *Practical Digital Photomicrography: Photography Through the Microscope for the Life Sciences*. Santa Barbara, CA: Rocky Nook Publishing, 2010.
An introduction to the techniques and equipment for taking digital photographs through a microscope.

Peres, Michael, and Andrew Peres. *Images from Science: An Exhibition of Scientific Photography*. Rochester, NY: Carey Graphic Arts Press, 2002.
This the catalog for a 2002 exhibition of scientific images.

Peres, Michael R. *Laboratory Imaging & Photography: Best Practices for Photomicrography & More*. Waltham, MA: Focal Press, 2016.
This book covers the standard procedures and approaches to laboratory photography.

ORGANIZATIONS

American Society of Picture Professionals
201 E 25th Street #11c
New York NY 10010
(516) 500-3686
Website: http://aspp.com
A nonprofit organization for anyone involved in the
photography professions, where members can
network, exchange ideas, and get industry news.

Society for Imaging Science & Photography
IS&T
7003 Kilworth Lane
Springfield, VA 22151
(703) 642-9090
Website: http://www.imaging.org/site/ist
A professional international organization dedicated
to educating members and others about the latest
scientific and technological developments in the field
of imaging.

BLOGS

Scientific American Compound Eye
http://blogs.scientificamerican.com/compound-eye
A blog about the many facets of science photography.

WEBSITES

Because of the changing nature of internet links, Rosen Publishing has developed an online list of websites related to the subject of this book. This site is updated regularly. Please use this link to access this list:

http://www.rosenlinks.com/CCWC/camera

GLOSSARY

BACKDROP A background or setting used as scenery for a movie, theater production, or photo shoot.

CANISTER A round or cylinder-shaped container, usually made of metal, that is used to store film.

CINEMATOGRAPHER The director of photography on a movie, responsible for all the artistic and technical decisions.

DOCUMENT To record something in written, photographic, digital, or other form.

ENHANCE To increase or improve something or raise it to a higher degree.

FOOTAGE A length of film made for movies or television.

FORENSIC Having to do with applying scientific techniques or methods to crime investigation.

INVOICE A bill for goods or services that have been provided.

LENS A piece of glass or other transparent substance with curved sides for concentrating or dispersing light waves, used in cameras and microscopes.

OBSERVATORY A room or building that holds an astronomical telescope.

PHYSICS The branch of science having to do with the nature and properties of matter and energy.

PORTFOLIO A set of drawings, paintings, or photographs that show a selection of someone's work.

PRODUCER The person responsible for managing all the aspects of a movie or television show.

REEL A cylinder that film is wound on.

RIGGING The ropes, wires, or other structures built to support people or equipment.

SCRUTINIZE To examine or inspect something closely and thoroughly.

SITTING A continuous period of being seated for a photograph or other portrait, or an appointment for a sitting.

TUITION The money charged by a school, college, or university for education and classes.

VENUE The place where an organized event, such as a conference, sporting event, or celebration, takes place.

VOCATIONAL Having to do with education or training specifically related to occupations or employment.

BIBLIOGRAPHY

Anonymous. "What Are the Duties of Telescope Operators at World-Class Observatories?" Quora.com, June 24, 2015. https://www.quora.com/What-are-the-duties-of-telescope-operators-at-world-class-observatories.

The Art Career Project. "Photojournalism Career—Tell a Story with Pictures." http://www.theartcareerproject.com/photojornalism/809.

Careerfinder.com. "Scientific Photographer." http://job-descriptions.careerplanner.com/Photographers-Scientific.cfm.

Career Igniter. "How to Become a Digital Colorist." http://www.careerigniter.com/careers/digital-colorist.

CBS This Morning. "'It's What I Do': A Photojournalist's Calling." CBS News, February 24, 2105. http://www.cbsnews.com/news/photojournalist-lynsey-addario-book-its-what-i-do-war-love-pregnancy-career.

CFNC.org. "Music Video Producer: What They Do." https://www1.cfnc.org/Plan/For_A_Career/Career_Profile/Career_Profile.aspx?id=MwQSHbd0XAP2FPAX07SDY5XAP2FPAXLhUa8AXAP3DPAXXAP3DPAX.

Creative Skillset. "Forensic Photographer." http://creativeskillset.org/job_roles/380_forensic_photographer.

Creative Skill Set. "Job Roles: Colourist." http://
creativeskillset.org/job_roles/3837_colourist.

CrimeSceneInvestigatorEdu.org. "What Is Forensic
Photography?" http://www
.crimesceneinvestigatoredu.org/csi-photographer.

FitzRoy, Maggie. "Crime Scene Technician's Job Nothing
Like You See on TV." Jacksonville.com, March 19, 2010.
http://jacksonville.com/community
/shorelines/2010-03-13/story/crime_scene
_technicians_job_nothing_like_you_see_on_tv_0#.

Harding, JG. "Adam Powell: How I Became a Music Video
Director." *Sound on Sound*, February 2011. http://www
.soundonsound.com/sos/feb11/articles
/adam-powell.htm.

Markusic, Mayflor. "Scientific Photography." Bright Hub,
May 25, 2009. http://www.brighthub.com/multimedia
/photography/articles/36246.aspx.

National Careers Service. "Job Profiles: Cinema
Projectionist." https://nationalcareersservice
.direct.gov.uk/advice/planning/jobprofiles/Pages
/cinemaprojectionist.aspx.

National Public Radio. "Seeing Stars: A Telescope Operator'
Night." *All Things Considered*, June 4, 2010.
http://www.npr.org/2010/06/04/127477503/seeing
-stars-a-telescope-operators-night.

Official Tom Cruise Blog. "How to Be a Film Grip on Movie Crews." November 11, 2012. http://www .tomcruise.com/blog/2012/11/01 /aspiring2actwritedirect-aspiring-series-aspiring -movie-grip-guide.

Robertson, Barbara. "The Colorists." CG Society, May 1, 2006. http://www.cgsociety.org/index.php /CGSFeatures/CGSFeatureSpecial/the_colorists.

Sokanu.com. "What Does a Motion Picture Projectionist Do?" https://www.sokanu.com/careers/motion- picture -projectionist.

Sonders, Douglas. "Simple Tips for Effectively Photographing Dogs in Studio." Fstoppers, January 29, 2015. https://fstoppers.com/animal/simple-tips -effectively-photographing-dogs-studio-56461.

Subbaraman, Nidhi. "Photographer Has Front-Row Seat for Big Scientific Discoveries." BetaBoston, June 10, 2015. http://www.betaboston.com /news/2015/06/10/photographer-has-front-row -seat-for-big-scientific-discoveries.

Williams, Ellie. "The Role of a Photographer Examiner in a Crime Scene." Chron.com. http://work.chron.com /role-photographer-examiner-crime-scene-14949 .html.

INDEX

ABOUT THE AUTHOR

Marcia Amidon Lusted has written extensively for young readers. She is also a former magazine editor and spent a lot of time working with photographers and finding appropriate photographs for publications. Learn more about her books at www.adventuresinnonfiction.com.

PHOTO CREDITS

Cover, p. 1 racorn/Shutterstock.com; pp. 4–5 Ilya Oreshkov/Shutterstock.com; pp. 8–9 Everett Historical/Shutterstock.com; p. 11 © iStockphoto.com/Juanmonino; pp. 12–13 Kanin.studio/Shutterstock.com; pp. 18–19 WEExp/Shutterstock.com; pp. 20–21 lightpoet/Shutterstock.com; p. 22 © iStockphoto.com/David H. Lewis; pp. 30–31 Connor Evans/Shutterstock.com; p. 32 Halfpoint/Shutterstock.com; p. 35 © iStockphoto.com/coloroftime; pp. 40–41 Pavel L Photo and Video/Shutterstock.com; pp. 42–43 philipimage/iStock/Thinkstock; p. 45 razihusin/Shutterstock.com; pp. 50–51 ishkov sergey/Shutterstock.com; pp. 52–53 taniavolobueva/Shutterstock.com; p. 55 DW labs Incorporated/Shutterstock.com; p. 62 Augustino/Shutterstock.com; p. 64 © AF archive/Alamy Stock Photo; p. 66 © Rex Features/AP Images; p. 73 © iStockphoto.com/vmaze pp. 74–75 © louise murray/Alamy Stock Photo; p. 78 milos-kreckovic/iStock/Thinkstock; pp. 84–85 © ITAR-TASS Photo Agency/Alamy Stock Photo; p. 86 © B Christopher/Alamy Stock Photo; pp. 88–89 John A Davis/Shutterstock.com; pp. 96–97 Corepics VOF/Shutterstock.com; pp. 100–101 © Ian Miles-Flashpoint Pictures/Alamy Stock Photo; p. 102 © Photos 12/Alamy Stock Photo; pp. 108–109 Scharfsinn/Shutterstock.com; p. 113 © Leo Francini/Alamy Stock Photo; pp. 114–115 © nikkytok/Shutterstock.com; interior pages graphic (camera) Naghiyev/Shutterstock.com.

Designer: Brian Garvey; Editor and Photo Researcher: Bethany Bryan